Your Government:
How It Works

The National Transportation Safety Board

Rich Mintzer

Chelsea House Publishers
Philadelphia

CHELSEA HOUSE PUBLISHERS
Editor in Chief Sally Cheney
Director of Production Kim Shinners
Creative Manager Takeshi Takahashi
Manufacturing Manager Diann Grasse

Staff for THE NATIONAL TRANSPORTATION SAFETY BOARD
Assistant Editor Susan Naab
Production Assistant Jaimie Winkler
Picture Researcher Jaimie Winkler
Series Designers Keith Trego, Takeshi Takahashi
Layout 21st Century Publishing and Communications, Inc.

The Chelsea House World Wide Web address is
http://www.chelseahouse.com

First Printing
1 3 5 7 9 8 6 4 2

Library of Congress Cataloging-in-Publication Data

Mintzer, Richard.
    The National Transportation Safety Board / by Rich Mintzer.
       p. cm. — (Your government—how it works)
Summary: Describes the workings and history of the National Transportation Safety Board as part of the United States government, including how it investigates transportation accidents and makes safety recommendations.
Includes bibliographical references and index.
    ISBN 0-7910-6794-7
    1. United States. National Transportation Safety Board. 2. Traffic safety—United States—Juvenile literature. 3. Transportation accidents—United States—Juvenile literature. [1. United States. National Transportation Safety Board. 2. Traffic safety. 3. Transportation accidents. 4. Accident investigation.] I. Title. II. Series.
HE5614.2 .M535 2002
363.12'56'0973—dc21
                                                    2002000044

Contents

YOUR GOVERNMENT: HOW IT WORKS

Introduction

Government: Crises of Confidence

Arthur M. Schlesinger, jr.

FROM THE START, Americans have regarded their government with a mixture of reliance and mistrust. The men who founded the republic understood the importance of government. "If men were angels," observed the 51st Federalist Paper, "no government would be necessary." But men are not angels. Because human beings are subject to wicked as well as to noble impulses, government was deemed essential to assure freedom and order.

The American revolutionaries, however, also knew that government could become a source of injury and oppression. The men who gathered in Philadelphia in 1787 to write the Constitution therefore had two purposes in mind: They wanted to establish a strong central authority and to limit that central authority's capacity to abuse its power.

To prevent the abuse of power, the Founding Fathers wrote two basic principles into the Constitution. The principle of federalism divided power between the state governments and the central authority. The principle of the separation of powers subdivided the central authority itself into three branches—the executive, the legislative, and the judiciary—so that "each may be a check on the other."

YOUR GOVERNMENT: HOW IT WORKS examines some of the major parts of that central authority, the federal government. It explains how various officials, agencies, and departments operate and explores the political

Introduction

organizations that have grown up to serve the needs of government.

The federal government as presented in the Constitution was more an idealistic construct than a practical administrative structure. It was barely functional when it came into being.

This was especially true of the executive branch. The Constitution did not describe the executive branch in any detail. After vesting executive power in the president, it assumed the existence of "executive departments" without specifying what these departments should be. Congress began defining their functions in 1789 by creating the Departments of State, Treasury, and War.

President Washington, assisted by Secretary of the Treasury Alexander Hamilton, equipped the infant republic with a working administrative structure. Congress also continued that process by creating more executive departments as they were needed.

Throughout the 19th century, the number of federal government workers increased at a consistently faster rate than did the population. Increasing concerns about the politicization of public service led to efforts—bitterly opposed by politicians—to reform it in the latter part of the century.

The 20th century saw considerable expansion of the federal establishment. More importantly, it saw growing impatience with bureaucracy in society as a whole.

The Great Depression during the 1930s confronted the nation with its greatest crisis since the Civil War. Under Franklin Roosevelt, the New Deal reshaped the federal government, assigning it a variety of new responsibilities and greatly expanding its regulatory functions. By 1940, the number of federal workers passed the 1 million mark.

Critics complained of big government and bureaucracy. Business owners resented federal regulation. Conservatives worried about the impact of paternalistic government on self-reliance, on community responsibility, and on economic and personal freedom.

When the United States entered World War II in 1941, government agencies focused their energies on supporting the war effort. By the end of World War II, federal civilian employment had risen to 3.8 million. With peace, the federal establishment declined to around 2 million in 1950. Then growth resumed, reaching 2.8 million by the 1980s.

A large part of this growth was the result of the national government assuming new functions such as: affirmative action in civil rights, environmental protection, and safety and health in the workplace.

Some critics became convinced that the national government was a steadily growing behemoth swallowing up the liberties of the people. The 1980s brought new intensity to the debate about government growth. Foes of Washington bureaucrats preferred local government, feeling it more responsive to popular needs.

But local government is characteristically the government of the locally powerful. Historically, the locally powerless have often won their human and constitutional rights by appealing to the national government. The national government has defended racial justice against local bigotry, upheld the Bill of Rights against local vigilantism, and protected natural resources from local greed. It has civilized industry and secured the rights of labor organizations. Had the states' rights creed prevailed, perhaps slavery would still exist in the United States.

Americans are still of two minds. When pollsters ask large, spacious questions—Do you think government has become too involved in your lives? Do you think government should stop regulating business?—a sizable majority opposes big government. But when asked specific questions about the practical work of government—Do you favor Social Security? Unemployment compensation? Medicare? Health and safety standards in factories? Environmental protection?—a sizable majority approves of intervention.

We do not like bureaucracy, but we cannot live without it. We need its genius for organizing the intricate details of our daily lives. Without bureaucracy, modern society would collapse. It would be impossible to run any of the large public and private organizations we depend on without bureaucracy's division of labor and hierarchy of authority. The challenge is to keep these necessary structures of our civilization flexible, efficient, and capable of innovation.

More than 200 years after the drafting of the Constitution, Americans still rely on government but also mistrust it. These attitudes continue to serve us well. What we mistrust, we are more likely to monitor. And government needs our constant attention if it is to avoid inefficiency, incompetence, and arbitrariness. Without our informed participation, it cannot serve us individually or help us as a people to attain the lofty goals of the Founding Fathers.

*A possible Fourth of July cele-
bration in the early part of the
20th Century (possibly 1910).
At that time, the main form of
ground transportation, apart
from the trains, was the horse
drawn carriage.*

CHAPTER 1

The Early Growth of Transportation in America

PLANES, TRAINS, AND automobiles are three things we see all the time and usually take for granted. But there was a time in early America when these were not the common modes of transportation. In fact, each of these, and other forms of transportation that we see today, developed slowly over a period of time. It was important for people, animals, and goods to be moved from one place to another by a safe method of transportation.

Vehicles needed to be sturdy, dependable, and easy to operate. The history of transportation in America includes a number of inventions that changed the way we get from place to place. As more types of transportation appeared, however, more accidents and injuries occurred, and it became increasingly important for attention to be given to safety.

Horses and Wagons

Early American settlers rode horses or rode in horse-drawn carriages to get from place to place. Two-wheeled passenger carriages were a very popular way of getting around in the 1700s. They were light-weight and horses could move at a steady pace. However, they were not very sturdy and could not carry much more than the passengers.

To carry more goods and passengers, the early settlers built large four-wheeled covered wagons called Conestoga wagons, named after the region in which they were first built in the eighteenth century—the region of Conestoga, Pennsylvania. These big wagons, like those seen in old Western movies, came in three different sizes and had brakes for stopping. They could carry six passengers, plus wheat, flour, grain, iron, wood, or any other type of supplies from town to town. They moved slowly along bumpy roads and occasionally tipped over when they hit a large rock or rounded a steep curve on the path. Wheels would break or the axles that hold the wheels together underneath the wagon would sometimes snap from the weight of a very heavy load. Another problem was that any transportation that was pulled by horses, donkeys, or other animals could move only if the animals were healthy, rested, and well fed. This meant that travelers had to stop to feed the animals and let them rest.

Steamboats and Railroads

The nineteenth century introduced several kinds of transportation. In 1786, John Fitch guided the first American-built, steam-powered boat along the Delaware River. Then, in 1807, American engineer and inventor Robert Fulton started passenger service along New York's Hudson River on his boat, *The Clermont*. It was the first steamboat used to carry passengers.

America's rivers were often called the nation's first highways. By the mid-nineteenth century, the large beautifully built steamboats were moving people and goods along these rivers throughout the nation. Steamboats could carry many passengers and were not slowed down by rough roads or steep hills. They did not move very quickly, but they were a relatively safe means of transportation.

Meanwhile, in Great Britain the railroad engine had been invented. By 1812, successful steam locomotives were being used, and by the 1820s Great Britain had a workshop made to build locomotives. In the United States, however, it would take much longer for the railroad to appear. Steep hills, rugged mountain ranges, thick forests, and many rivers and streams to cross made it more difficult to build railroads in America.

The first railroad locomotive to be assembled in the United States was the Stourbridge Lion. The engine had been brought over from England to be used on a railroad that would carry coal from the mines to a canal where it was to be loaded onto boats. The Stourbridge Lion was one of two locomotives built in 1829. When these locomotives were finished, each weighed nearly seven tons. This proved to be too heavy for the American railroad tracks, which had sharper curves than those in England. The two locomotives were stored and never used.

Railroad builders did not give up. A lightweight locomotive called the Tom Thumb was invented in 1830. It was

The steamboat (background) replaced the flatboat (foreground) as carrier of goods and people. The earliest steamboat technology dates back to 1786 when John Fitch navigated the first one of its kind down the Delaware River.

used to carry 36 passengers from Maryland to Ohio. Shortly after, a completely American-built steam engine called the Best Friend went into scheduled passenger service in Charleston, South Carolina. It pulled two train cars filled with 40 passengers at 29 miles per hour. Even at that slow speed, the train had several accidents, including a boiler explosion that killed one of the train workers and ended the run of the Best Friend.

Railroad companies tried many times to find an engine that had enough power to pull several cars full of cargo and passengers and that was also safe. Finally, by the middle of the 1800s, the railroad became a popular type of trans-portation. By the end of the 1800s, many railroads were taking people all over the young country of America. The many railroads helped in the building of towns and cities. Trains also carried building materials as well as food, animals, and cargo. People were able to settle in new territories and ride the railroads to get from place to place. However, more railroad travel meant more safety problems. Trains going too fast or not following their schedule led to train accidents. Another problem caused by more railroads was the need for a major supply of coal. This meant that more coal miners had to work in coal mines, which were dangerous places to work. There was also the problem of more **pollution.** Although it was not called pollution at the time, the thick clouds of smoke that were released into the air from the trains' steam engines were a major source of air polution.

While railroads stretched across the land, the late 1800s saw another means of transportation in many major cities. Trolleys and cable cars first appeared. The earliest trolleys were horse-drawn and moved slowly along main streets. Then, later on, trolleys were run by cables buried just beneath the surface of the streets. By the turn of the twentieth century, there were so many trolleys that trolley traffic jams frequently occurred in large cities like Cleveland and Philadelphia.

The very first automobile powered by the internal combustion engine was constructed in 1893 by Charles and Frank Duryea. People referred to it as a "horseless buggy."

The increased number of trolleys also led to many trolley car injuries. These were generally caused by too many people trying to ride on one trolley car at the same time, or by people being hit by one trolley car as they ran to catch another. Even if they weren't the safest means of transportation, they were very popular ways of getting to and from work. In fact, by the time World War I ended in 1918, trolleys were so popular that over 100,000 people worked for trolley companies, making it the fifth largest business in the country.

Automobiles

While trolleys, railroads, steamboats, and horse and carriages all were popular types of transportation in the United States, across the Atlantic Ocean in Europe the automobile had been invented. A new engine, called the **internal combustion engine**, had also been invented in Europe, and it would become the engine that powered automobiles.

In 1892, Charles and Frank Duryea built the first American-made automobile. It was nothing more than a horse buggy with a motor underneath. It took nearly nine hours to go just 50 miles, which meant it was traveling not much more than five miles per hour. However, it was the beginning of something big. The automobile was very appealing. It allowed people to travel on land without relying on animals. Also, unlike trains and steamships, which had a schedule and a route to follow, the automobile could take people anywhere they wanted to go at any time.

Just after the start of the 1900s, the automobile started to catch on. Ransom Eli Olds created the original Oldsmobile and sold nearly 10,000 by 1904. Cars went just slightly faster than horse-drawn carriages, but they didn't get tired or need to stop for food. There were, however, many problems with the early cars. Tires did not last very long, axles broke often, and gasoline sometimes caused fires. Also, many roads were bumpy and steering a car was difficult. There were many accidents. Laws were quickly created to try to keep drivers from running into each other, but not many drivers even knew what the laws were. It didn't matter if the early automobiles had problems, they were very popular with the wealthy people who could afford them.

Meanwhile, a young man named Henry Ford, born in 1863 in Michigan, was developing a strong interest in the automobile. At the age of 13, he had seen his first-ever steam engine traveling under its own power. Ford was fascinated and studied the engine closely. He was determined that he would create his own **self-propelled** vehicle. While working at his own invention, Ford met one of America's greatest inventors, Thomas Edison. Edison and Ford became friends, and Edison would not let Ford give up on his invention.

After trying eight different models, Ford invented the Model T. The car was first sold in 1908 and became the hottest-selling car for nearly 20 years. The Model T was not fancy, but it was made from parts that could be replaced if broken. Ford also invented the first **assembly line** for making these cars piece by piece. This rapid production of many cars at one time allowed Ford to sell cars for less money. Suddenly everyone could afford to own a car, not

just the wealthy. Cars became very popular, and other companies started to make them as well. At one time over 300 car companies were open for business. Most of these companies failed because they could not make a car that was safe enough to drive, was cheap enough to afford, and did not break down.

Just because there were many cars being built did not mean they were getting easier to drive. Most early cars had to be started by turning a crank in the front. Steering wheels did not always turn as quickly as the driver wanted them to and breaks did not always work either. There were no such things as seatbelts, air bags, or safety features. In the 1920s, there were more accidents than registered drivers. It still didn't seem to matter. Cars continued to become more popular than ever before, and by the end of the 1920s there were thousands of cars crowding the streets of every major city and small town.

Henry Ford perfected the Duryeas' "horseless buggy" in 1896. Here he sits in his "quadracycle" in front of his Michigan workshop. Ford would enlarge his automobile model to create the "Model T," which would become the best selling car in America for twenty years straight!

Brothers Orville and Wilbur Wright began working on the first successful airplane in 1900. Here they experiment with a glider in North Carolina.

Airplanes

Shortly after cars became the most popular mode of ground transportation, the airplane was introduced, which enabled people to travel through the skies. In 1900, the Wright brothers, Wilbur and Orville, of Dayton, Ohio, began their attempts to create the first airplane. First, they started with unmanned **gliders**, and then progressed to gliders with one of the Wright brothers on board. As an early safety precaution, the brothers flew their gliders along the beach where they could land, or crash, in the soft sand. Until that time, only hot air balloons had successfully carried a person off the ground.

By 1901, Orville and Wilbur Wright were very frustrated, having been unable to improve upon their early, unmanned gliders. Wilbur once told his brother, "Not within a thousand years would man ever fly." One year later, he was proved wrong. In 1902, the Wright brothers not only created a better glider, but they made one that a person could ride on and control.

Then in 1903, the Wrights made history. On December 17, 1903 they lifted off on the first motorized flying machine. The first flight lasted only 12 seconds, and the next couple of flights didn't last much longer. Still, this was the beginning of the airplane.

Improvements in air travel were made by daring pilots over the next several years. In 1923, the first U.S. coast-to-coast flight was made. It took almost 27 hours. Then in 1927, Charles Lindbergh flew his plane, *Spirit of St. Louis*, across the Atlantic Ocean. He left from New York and after 33 hours landed safely in Paris, France. The public was fascinated by Lindbergh's accomplishment. Suddenly everyone was interested in flying.

Airplanes had been used by both the United States and Germany in World War I, but mostly for transporting cargo or as military planes. The United States Post Office had begun transporting mail by airplane as far back as 1918. But it was not until the late 1920s and early1930s that passenger airplanes began operating. United Airlines, American Airlines, Trans World Airlines (TWA), and Pan American Airlines (Pan Am) were among the first major airline companies that opened for business. There were still only a few passenger planes available. One such plane was the DC-3, which was built to carry both the mail and 21 passengers. The DC-3s had both seats and sleeping berths, which were like beds where a few people could sleep during long distance flights. Still, not many people were brave enough to fly.

It would be several more years before airplanes became a popular type of transportation for passengers. Cars, however, were rapidly replacing the railroad as the leading means of ground transportation in the 1920s. Americans loved having cars, but with more cars came a need for greater safety.

The autobahn in Germany was one of the world's first state-of-the-art motorways. The highway links the German cities of Frankfurt and Manheim.

CHAPTER 2

The Need for Safer Transportation

THE NATIONAL CONFERENCE on Street and Highway Safety was organized in 1924 by the Secretary of Commerce, Herbert Hoover, who later became the 31st president of the United States. Members from every state were invited to discuss ways to reduce the number of accidents on streets and highways. This committee would meet in 1924, 1926, and 1930, and its goal was to come up with new safety laws and regulations for automobile travel. The meetings concluded with local governments in towns and cities being put in charge of making their own traffic laws.

By 1931, each state had many new traffic laws. There were also many more cars on the roads. The new cars had better brakes and were easier to steer. Unfortunately, more drivers and faster cars meant more serious accidents. In 1931, nearly 33,500 people were killed in automobile accidents. It was estimated that another 1 million people were injured. During the 10-year period from 1920 to 1930, motor vehicle accidents had more than doubled. The problem was that the traffic laws were different in every town, and many drivers still did not know the laws.

Clearly, the time had come for the formulation of standard rules regarding speed limits, passing other cars, making U-turns, and so on that all drivers would follow. States would be required to post traffic signs and make sure that drivers knew the rules before receiving a license. The government also needed to begin regulating how cars were made. Steering wheels, headlights, engines, and other parts of each automobile had to meet certain requirements before a car could be sold. As a result, the Uniform Vehicle Code was written to ensure that all drivers were licensed and that all vehicles were inspected for safety.

Soon, each state had established clear laws and regulations for drivers. The federal government watched over the state laws and made sure that car manufacturers met certain standards when building cars. During the 1930s, automobile associations, auto clubs, and safety councils also started teaching people about safe driving.

Improvement of Roads

While the laws and regulations made driving safer in the mid 1930s, there were still more and more cars crowding the roads. This created a need for wider roads that could handle more cars and trucks. States, and the federal government, began making plans to build highways. One of the models for American highways was the German autobahn, which opened in 1935. The autobahn was a paved highway that allowed cars to travel faster than they could on local roads. A government organization called the Bureau of Public Roads studied the possibilities of building these new highways. They wanted to charge drivers a toll for riding on the new roads. The money from the tolls would pay for the cost of maintaining the highways. At this time, the United States was going through the Great Depression, which began in 1929 with the crash of the stock market. Many people were out of work. Besides making travel easier and safer, building new highways could provide many new jobs.

By the end of the 1930s, major highways were being planned. On April 27, 1939, President Roosevelt recommended that Congress consider action on a "special system of direct **interregional** highways, with connections through and around cities." Congress took up the recommendation, and the stage was set for highway building in America.

However, although some new highways were built in the 1940s, production on these important roads slowed down quickly. The United States had entered World War II, and manpower and money for building such highways was limited. It wasn't until the 1950s that many major highways began connecting the country. More highways helped people get places faster and helped trucks deliver goods to more cities and towns. However, highways also meant more high-speed travel, and once again there was a concern for greater automobile safety.

Automobile Safety Measures

In 1953, the Colorado State Medical Society, made up of doctors, wrote a paper in which they suggested a new safety devise for automobiles. They called the new idea lap belts and suggested that these belts be built into every automobile. But like many great ideas, it took several years until anyone paid attention. In 1955, the Society of Automobile Engineers (car makers) set up a committee to study the idea of seatbelts. Then in 1956, Ford and Chrysler, two of the biggest car manufacturers

Volvo was the first auto company to install cross-chest belts in 1956. Here we see Commerce Secretary Luther Hodges adjusting his seat belt in 1961. He ordered all Commerce Department vehicles to also install this type of safety belt.

in America, began offering lap belts in the front seats of their cars. The belts were offered as an option, which meant that drivers could choose to have them if they wanted, or decline their inclusion. Most drivers did not choose to buy the new safety feature. In 1956, Volvo became the first car maker to offer cross-chest seatbelts as an option. Like many new inventions, however, the cross-chest seatbelt did not catch on immediately. In fact, it took more than 20 years and thousands of unnecessary injuries and deaths before seatbelts were placed in every car and wearing them became the law.

Airplane Safety Measures

Not only were there safety concerns about cars, but airplane travel also needed to be safe. As far back as 1926, the Air Commerce Act was passed by Congress to regulate air travel. At that time leaders in the airline industry were aware that there would be rapid growth in air travel in the future as planes became safer and more airports opened. They wanted the government to improve and maintain safety standards. This act put the Secretary of Commerce in charge of making air traffic rules, certifying aircrafts to make sure that they were safe and that pilots had licenses.

In 1934, the Aeronautics Branch of the Department of Commerce became the Bureau of Air Commerce. The bureau soon opened the first centers for **air traffic control** (ATC). The early air traffic controllers used blackboards, maps, and handwritten charts to make sure that planes were not too close to each other when traveling from one destination to another.

By the 1940s, two federal agencies were needed to handle the number of planes flying. The Civil Aeronautics Administration (CAA) was set up to make sure the planes were inspected for safety. The Civil Aeronautics Board (CAB) was set up to make safety rules and investigate accidents.

A horrible collision over the Grand Canyon on June 30, 1956 between a TWA passenger plane and a United Airlines passenger plane, which killed 128 passengers, prompted the federal government to form a federal aviation administration to oversee airline safety. After this tragedy, the FAA would be founded by the Federal Aviation Administration Act of 1958.

By the 1950s, flying had indeed "taken off." Every major city now had an airport, and all major airlines handled many daily flights. Several mid-air collisions made the headlines in the 1950s, including one dramatic collision over the Grand Canyon. On June 30, 1956, a TWA passenger plane and a United Airlines passenger plane collided in mid-air over the canyon, killing all 128 people aboard the two planes. This was one of the reasons for the Federal Aviation Act of 1958, which marked the beginning of the Federal Aviation Administration (FAA).

Among the many responsibilities of the Federal Aviation Administration was enforcing safety rules and regulations. The Federal Aviation Administration would soon find that it was involved with many other issues such as noise reduction and airplane inspections.

By the mid 1960s, the Federal Aviation Administration had even more responsibilities, including **hijackings**. The Civil Aeronautics Board was still in charge of investigating accidents but also had the busy job of handling how the money was spent in the airline industry. It was necessary for one bureau strictly devoted to accident investigation. This would take the burden off the Federal Aviation Administration and Civil Aeronautics Board. It would also provide the country with one central investigative organization to handle major ground transportation and boating accidents. Most important, this would be an independent organization that could not be controlled by political leaders or manufacturers.

The Civil Aeronautics Board's bureau of safety was the model for the National Transportation Safety Board, which was created in 1967.

*On Saturday May 11, 1996 a
ValuJet plane crashed in the
Florida Everglades, killing all
109 passengers. The NTSB vice
chairman, Robert Francis (right),
held a news conference to
inform the public about the
crash. He is escorted here
by Luiz Fernandez (left),
who was with the Metro
Dade Fire Department.*

CHAPTER 3

The National Transportation Safety Board: How It Works

IN 1967, THE National Transportation Safety Board (NTSB) was established to help watch over all transportation and find ways to make it safer. Originally, the NTSB relied on the Department of Transportation for money and support. Then, in 1975, they broke all connections with the Department of Transportation and became an independent agency.

From the beginning, the U.S. Congress put the NTSB in charge of investigating all airline accidents in the United States. The board was also asked to investigate major highway, railroad, marine, and pipeline accidents. In addition, investigators from the board would be sent to foreign countries if a United States plane or ship were involved in an accident anywhere in the world. On call 24 hours per day, 365 days a year, NTSB investigators would be ready to investigate an accident and try to determine why it occurred.

Once they arrive on the scene, the highly trained NTSB experts are expected to investigate every possible cause of the accident and take detailed notes. After an investigation is completed, the NTSB would determine what is called "probable cause," or the most likely reason why the accident happened. The board then publishes a report that explains what they believe caused the accident. Finally, recommendations are made to help prevent such accidents from happening again.

Investigation of Accidents

The study of many accidents allows the NTSB to discover certain accident patterns. For example, if the same model of automobile were involved in several similar accidents in different parts of the country, then the board might check to see if something was made incorrectly by the automobile manufacturer. Another example might show a pattern of accidents involving bus drivers who had been driving shifts of ten hours or more. After studying the cause of the accidents, the NTSB might conclude that the drivers were too tired to drive so many hours without taking a break. The board would then recommend new rules for drivers. Such rules might limit drivers to five or six hours of driving before needing to take a break.

Along with studying accidents, the NTSB also keeps track of how well safety features are working. For example, the NTSB might study such things as car seats for young children or seatbelts to see whether these devices are helping to prevent injuries. If safety seats for young children were not preventing many injuries, the board might make recommendations to the manufacturer about ways to make them safer. The NTSB cannot make laws or tell manufacturers how they must build their vehicles or safety equipment. However, they can make important suggestions based on what they have learned. Over the years since the NTSB was established, 80% of their recommendations have been followed by transportation manufacturers and by the government agencies that make and enforce safety laws.

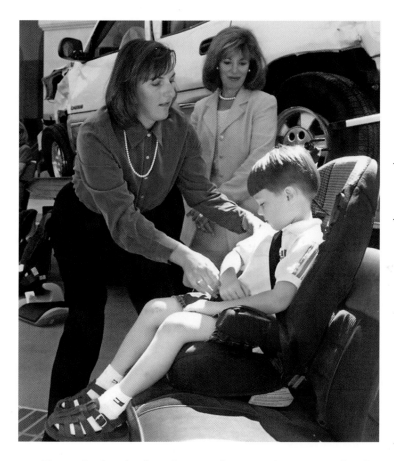

One of the duties of the NTBS is to monitor the effectiveness of safety prevention efforts and test new safety ideas. Here we see a news conference at which an emergency room nurse is strapping in four-year-old Kyle DeWitt to a child safety seat. The news conference on August 8, 2000 was prompted by new legislation proposed in California that would require children six years of age and under or under sixty pounds to be placed in a child safety seat.

From the beginning, it was also very important for the NTSB to be set up to act independently. This way no other company or organization could tell them how to conduct their investigations. NTSB investigators could figure out exactly what caused an accident without anyone else interfering with their investigation. This does not mean that the NTSB works completely alone. Sometimes pilots or engineers are called on to help answer tough questions about how a certain type of plane should be flown or how a train should be engineered. The NTSB might call on an expert in a certain area if they believe the expert can help them come to an understanding of what caused an accident. Often the FAA or the United States Coast Guard helps with an investigation.

The NTSB promotes safety by providing fliers and booklets to the public that explain the recent findings of their safety studies and investigations. They make general recommendations to the public, as we see on this "Please Drive Safely" sign. The NTSB also holds seminars and workshops for the public to spread the word about safety.

Although it does not happen very often, the NTSB does find some instances in which criminal activity was involved in a transportation incident. If the investigators find that someone deliberately caused a crash, they will turn over the case to the Federal Bureau of Investigation (FBI). The NTSB will help by reporting their findings, but the FBI will have to track down the criminals.

Once the NTSB completes an investigation or makes safety recommendations, it provides information to the public. The board prints fliers and booklets for people to read about safety. They also conduct seminars and workshops on safety. The NTSB tries to spread the word about their findings to as many people as possible so that the lessons learned from one accident can be used to prevent future tragedies. Because the board openly communicates important safety information to the public, the American people have come to trust the reports of the NTSB.

Agencies such as the Federal Aviation Administration, Department of Transportation, Federal Railroad Administration, Federal Transit Administration, National Highway Traffic Safety Administration, and the U.S. Coast Guard all receive recommendations about how to make travel safer.

By working with these agencies to help establish new rules and regulations, the NTSB acts as a watchdog, keeping track of the safety of millions of Americans as they travel.

Assistance for Accident Victims

In addition to investigating accidents and making safety regulations, the NTSB assists the families of crash victims. On October 9, 1996, President Bill Clinton signed the Aviation Disaster Family Assistance Act into law. The law states that the NTSB, and the airline company, must take action to help the families of the people involved in an airplane accident. The NTSB has set up a Family Affairs Division, which looks at the needs of these families affected by serious accidents.

NTSB as Judges in Accidents

Another function of the NTSB is to serve as judges. The Federal Aviation Administration and the U.S. Coast Guard oversee all air and boat travel in the United States. Often, after an accident, a pilot or ship captain is in danger of having his or her license or certification taken away. The person can ask the NTSB to review the case and act as a judge in the matter. It is very important for anyone piloting a plane or sailing a boat to have the proper skills to operate the vehicle and to understand all the laws and regulations involved.

The NTSB can review the situation and help decide whether the pilot or ship captain was at fault or not. Decisions made by the NTSB can still be appealed in the Federal Court of Appeals, which means they can be taken to a court of law to get another decision. However, when such cases have been taken into a court of law, 90% of the time the courts agree with the decision that was made by the NTSB.

It is important for the NTSB not to take on too many other responsibilities. The board needs to focus as much time and attention as possible on their number one goal: safer transportation for everyone—on land, in the air, and on the water.

*A member of the NTSB, Arnold
Scott (left), and Bob Wilden, aircraft mechanic, use the engine of
a restored World War II aircraft
to uncover the reasons for an air
crash that occurred on August 25,
2001 in Raton, New Mexico.*

CHAPTER 4

Investigating Accidents: The Go-Team

SINCE 1967, THE NTSB has investigated over 110,000 airline accidents, and thousands of car, train, and boat accidents. As the world's leading accident investigators, the NTSB is the first organization called upon when an airplane accident occurs.

The Go-Team

The first step of an NTSB investigation is putting together a Go-Team. The Go-Team is made up of people who are experts in investigating accidents. Working just like trained detectives, these team members investigate every possible clue that might lead to the cause of the accident.

The NTSB has many investigators ready to go at any time. Go-Team members are always ready to pack their bags and head out the door. They carry flashlights, tape recorders, and cameras, along with plenty of audiotapes and rolls of film. Sometimes they take along such tools as screwdrivers in case they have to open and study parts from the vehicle involved in the accident. Each Go-Team is led by a senior NTSB investigator, who has considerable years of experience. Depending on the size of the accident and how much needs to be investigated, the team consists of three people to fifteen or more.

Each member of the team has certain responsibilities. For example, in an airline accident, one member might be in charge of investigating the scene of the accident to determine where the parts of the plane landed, how hard they hit the ground, and at what angles they fell. Another investigator might be in charge of interviewing witnesses who saw the accident. This way he or she can get details about what might have happened.

One Go-Team member will have the important job of investigating the communication between the pilot and the air traffic control tower. Pilots are always talking with air traffic controllers on the ground. The air traffic controllers help guide the pilots along the path of their flight and tell them about weather conditions and other important things they need to know to fly safely. This team member will learn what was being said between the pilot and the control tower before the crash.

Another Go-Team member will be in charge of investigating what is called *human performance*. This is an investigation of the person who was either flying the plane, engineering the train, or steering the car or boat. This Go-Team member will investigate to determine if the person was too tired, taking medication, or drinking alcohol.

A team member is usually put in charge of studying the weather conditions, especially when it involves an airplane accident. Another team member will be in charge of investigating the physical safety of the plane itself. For example, he or she will check to see when the plane was last inspected

The black box provides valuable information to NTSB investigators working to uncover the cause of an accident. The very strongly constructed box can withstand the excessive forces of a crash, as well as the excessive heat and water that might be associated with a crash. Here we see NTSB investigators carrying a black box from Egypt Air Flight 990 that was found 270 feet under water. All 217 passengers on board the flight died in the accident.

to make sure all parts were working.

Team members do not have to work alone. Each Go-Team specialist may put together a smaller team of his or her own. They can include people from outside the NTSB to help them. For example, a team member might ask for help in the investigation from an expert who repairs airplane engines. A local meteorologist, or weatherman, might be called on to discuss what the weather conditions were like in the area at the time of the accident.

Usually, while the investigation is taking place, one member of the NTSB team will act as a **spokesperson** to talk with members of the media about what the team has learned. In airline accidents, for example, the spokesperson announces when the **black box** has been found. This is a very important part of the investigation process, because the black box often helps the team figure out why the accident occurred. The box itself is so strong that it can usually withstand even a crash. Inside is a recording device that is used to record everything that is said by the crew before the crash. The pilot or a crewmember may have mentioned on the tape that something was wrong with the plane. In a hijacking, other voices may be heard when the hijackers try to take over the plane. The NTSB has a special technical laboratory in which they are able to listen to voice recorders, not only for planes but also for boats and trains.

Accident Reports

There is no set time as to how long an investigation must last. NTSB investigations last as long as it takes to find out why the accident occurred. This could be a few days, a couple of months, or several years, depending on the type of accident. Usually, the investigation at the scene of the accident lasts only a few days.

Sometimes parts of an airliner are taken to another location so the plane can be put back together piece by piece. This allows the investigators to get an idea of how one part of the plane might have caused another to catch fire or explode. For instance, when TWA Flight 800 suddenly exploded over Long Island Sound (New York) in 1996, the parts of the plane were taken out of the water and put together in an old airline hanger on Long Island. There, Go-Team members could study them more carefully.

Finally, every investigation moves to central NTSB headquarters in Washington D.C., where team members review all the information they have gathered. Like putting together a giant jigsaw puzzle, the investigators pool all their information to figure out exactly how and why the accident occurred. When they are convinced that they have determined the reason for the accident, they start putting together a report, which explains exactly how they believe the accident occurred. A major accident report is filed for larger accidents, such as the crash of a large plane. Included in the report will be:

- The facts, explaining what took place on that day

- The conditions, including the weather

- The circumstances around the accident, such as where the plane was headed and how many passengers were on board

- Analysis of all the information

- The conclusion reached by the team regarding how the accident occurred

Investigation reports are published for all major accidents. They are made available to the public so that anyone can read about how the accident occurred.

The NTSB also writes "accident briefs," which are much smaller reports on all small accidents that are investigated. These reports include a short summary of how and why an accident occurred.

Another report is prepared every year for the United States Congress. This lets Congress review the work of the NTSB. The reports to Congress include major accident investigations. Also included are important recommendations of the NTSB for changes in transportation safety. The reports are available for the public to read so they can also learn exactly what the NTSB has done over the past year. Taxpayer dollars support the NTSB. Despite the fact that most people do not like paying taxes, there is rarely ever a complaint about funding for this important organization. Incredibly, it costs only about 25 cents per person per year to maintain the National Transportation Safety Board.

Among the many accidents that the NTSB has investigated were the airplane crashes that killed celebrities John Denver in 1997 and John F. Kennedy, Jr. in 1999, as well as the famous Exxon Valdez oil spill in 1989, which dumped more than 11 million gallons of crude oil into the waters off the coast of Alaska. The NTSB was also involved in investigating the tragic events of September 11, 2001 (although the FBI actually headed the investigation because it involved hijackers).

Almost two months after the September 11, 2001 attack on the World Trade Center buildings, American Airlines Flight 587 crashed in the Belle Harbor neighborhood of Queens, New York. More than 250 passengers and nine crew members died in the accident. Understandably, Americans and the rest of the world feared it might be the work of terrorists.

CHAPTER 5

Investigating Flight 587

TO GET A clear idea of what takes place in an investigation, let's take a look at the early part of a recent investigation involving the crash of American Airlines Flight 587. Included here is only some of the long and detailed work done by the NTSB Go-Team in response to this recent tragedy.

It was a clear morning on November 13, 2001—almost two months to the day, after the tragic terrorist attacks on the World Trade Center— when Flight 587 took off from Kennedy airport in New York City. Bound for the Dominican Republic, the flight was scheduled to leave at 8:40 A.M. The plane took off almost 30 minutes later at 9:14 A.M. Three minutes after take-off, at 9:17 A.M, the plane came crashing down on several houses just five miles from the airport. Over 250 passengers and nine crewmembers were killed.

Witnesses saw parts of the plane falling off moments before the crash. Several pieces of the plane landed on private homes, setting them on fire. One of the two engines came crashing down in a gas station, where it landed only a few feet away from the gas pumps. The other engine crashed through a boat parked in a driveway.

Go-Team Begins

Within minutes after the crash, while 44 fire trucks and 200 fire fighters raced to the scene, the NTSB was assembling a Go-Team. The team of special investigators were to head to New York City immediately for an investigation. Because of the terrorist attacks of September 11, many people feared that this could be another terrorist attack.

Then-Mayor Rudy Giuliani put New York City on high-alert against terrorist activities. All the nearby airports were closed. Many roads in and out of the city were also closed. Everyone waited for the NTSB investigation to begin.

At the start of the investigation, there was no reason to suspect terrorism. There had been no terrorist threats and no suspicious passengers seen boarding the plane. Therefore, the NTSB took charge of the investigation, as the city, the nation, and the world nervously waited to see what they found.

The Go-Team started investigating all possible clues that might tell them what caused this horrible crash. Jim Hall, former chairman of the NTSB, told reporters that there would probably be several hundred pieces of information about the operation of that aircraft. The Go-Team would need to investigate as many of these pieces of information as they could find.

Investigators were very busy on the November morning of the crash. They met with the air traffic controllers at Kennedy Airport to investigate all communication between the pilot and the control tower. With the help of the U.S. Coast Guard, they checked out rumors that the

plane had dumped fuel into the water just before the crash. No such fuel was found. Team members also looked to see when the plane was last inspected. They wanted to make sure all parts were in working order. A top spokesperson from American Airlines told the NTSB that the plane recently had a maintenance check and that a more complete check of all of the parts had been done just over one month earlier. He also explained that the 37-minute delay in take-off was not because of any **mechanical problems.**

At 1:30 P.M., just over four hours after the crash of Flight 587, the NTSB held a **news conference,** where they met with reporters from many newspapers and television stations. Marion Blakely, NTSB chairwoman, announced that the investigative teams had recovered the flight data recorder, the black box, from the plane. It was being flown back to Washington, D.C., where experts would take it to the special NTSB laboratory to listen to the voice recording of the pilot and co-pilot prior to the crash.

Only four hours after the crash of American Airlines Flight 587 on Tuesday, November 13, 2001, the black box had been retrieved and a press conference was held by the NTSB. Behind the podium we see NTSB lead investigator George Black and NTSB chairman Marion Blakely at a Holiday Inn near John F. Kennedy International Airport in Queens, New York.

Possible Mechanical Problems

By the end of the day, the NTSB was investigating the possibility that the crash was due to a serious engine problem. They had not ruled out other possibilities, but their clues indicated that something had gone wrong with the plane and that this was not the work of terrorists.

The next morning, George Black of the NTSB went on ABC television's *Good Morning America*. He explained that the two engines had been found: one at a gas station and the other in a driveway where a boat had been parked. Both of these engines were taken to another location, where experts could examine them carefully. Later that day, in an interview with CNN television news network, Black said that the NTSB teams were also going to look at the radar information from local airports that were following the **flight pattern** of the plane. All airports use radar to keep track of which planes are in the sky and to make sure no other planes get too close to one another. The radar information about Flight 587 would not only show the plane in flight but would also show when pieces started falling off.

While the teams in New York City continued their investigation, the black box flight recorder arrived in Washington, D.C. The recordings were played. The only voices were those of the pilot and co-pilot. Nothing sounded out of the ordinary. The fact that no other voices were on the tape indicated that this did not appear to be a hijacking. Marion Blakely contacted FBI director Robert Mueller to let him know that there was still no evidence of any criminal activity.

Later that day, it was revealed to the media that the type of engine on Flight 587 had been investigated by the NTSB before. The plane engines were made by the General Electric Company. Almost one year earlier, the NTSB had asked the FAA to review repairs made on that type of engine. This recommendation was made after an engine caught fire while repairs were being made on a U.S. Airways aircraft.

A year before that, the NTSB had made another

This is the fire-damaged flight data recorder from American Airlines Flight 587. Because the recorder was severely damaged, it made the task of obtaining the information more difficult. There were several theories presented by the NTSB as to why Flight 587 crashed into the peaceful Queens neighbor-hood, plunging America and the world into a fresh state of panic.

recommendation about a plane with the same type of engine. The recommendation was to improve the fire detection system in the engine so that there would be an early warning in the event of a fire. This recommendation came after an engine fire on an American Airlines flight, which took off from Puerto Rico.

The NTSB warnings were not ignored. The FAA told the airline companies to closely examine the parts of these engines. General Electric also followed the NTSB instruction and studied the engines more carefully. However, they had not found anything that needed to be changed in the engines.

Meanwhile, the investigation of Flight 587 continued. Later the next day, a second black box recorder was found. This second recorder is a **flight data recorder**. It keeps track of the actions of the engine and the instruments used to fly the plane. For example, a piloting error or an improperly working engine would show up on the record kept by this device. The flight data recorder was also taken by the NTSB for further study.

Possible Problems with Birds

While the team was considering the many possible problems that might have caused the engines to fall from the plane, another problem was being explored by other team members working at the airport. Kennedy Airport sits right along side of a bay, where many birds often fly or land close to the runways. Investigators were now looking into the possibility that the engines might have sucked in several birds as the plane taxied down the runway. Possibly, birds caused the engines to catch fire.

Possible Wake Turbulence

Thursday, three days after the crash, investigators started talking about yet another possible cause of the accident. This one appeared to be the most likely cause. By studying the flight records, investigators learned that Flight 587 took off less than two minutes after the plane ahead of it took off. Multiple planes waiting in line for take off are supposed to stagger their take off times by at least two minutes. In the case of Flight 587, however, investigators determined that the plane took off fifteen seconds too soon.

When planes take off, and when they fly, they create a strong wind that pushes back behind them, sometimes called a wake. The wind from the aircraft in front of Flight 587, a much larger Japanese plane, may have caused what is called **wake turbulence**, which may have affected Flight 587. Wake turbulence is a very strong swirling wind almost like a small tornado. Since Flight 587 took off too soon, it was too close to the plane in front of it, and the high winds of the wake turbulence ripped part of the tail section off the plane. This made it impossible for the pilots to steer Flight 587 and resulted in the crash.

While wake turbulence appeared to be the most probable cause of the crash, all the many possible reasons for the accident would still be carefully explored for the next several months. The NTSB would not make a final decision on the cause of the accident until very certain of being correct. In the meantime, they would work closely with the families of the many victims to make sure that they were being taken care of in their time of loss and sadness. The NTSB would also make recommendations regarding anything they found that could be improved for the future safety of passengers. The NTSB has made many recommendations over the years. These recommendations come from investigations just like the one conducted on Flight 587.

On October 3, 2001 Greyhound
bus service was suspended
temporarily after a fatal bus crash
in Tennessee. In Minneapolis,
Minnesota, seen in this photo-
graph, passengers await their
bus departure during the emer-
gency pause in service.

CHAPTER 6

Making Safety Recommendations

NTSB INVESTIGATIONS LEAD to the most probable cause of an accident. The next step is to try to make sure that the same type of accident does not happen again. This is why the NTSB makes recommendations to the manufacturers of planes, trains, railroads, boats, and automobiles. They also make recommendations to the agencies that make the laws and those that regulate how vehicles are built and operated. In addition, the NTSB makes recommendations to the makers of safety equipment.

The NTSB spends many hours doing research before making a safety recommendation. When the board has determined a way of making transportation safer, they write a recommendation letter and send it to the proper agency or manufacturer. If, for example, an investigation of a bus accident shows that people were injured because the seats were built too close to one another, the NTSB will write a letter to the bus manufacturer and recommend that the seats be spaced farther apart. The board will explain the reasons for this recommendation citing an accident as an example.

Each recommendation letter is written for two reasons. First, the letter explains the safety measures the bureau feels are necessary. Second, the letter describes the accident or accidents that led to this recommendation.

A typical recommendation letter might begin with the following introduction:

Mr. John Smith
Chairman of Acme Bus Manufacturing

Dear Mr. Smith:

The National Transportation Safety Board is an independent federal agency charged by Congress with investigating transportation accidents, determining their probable cause and making recommendations to prevent similar accidents from occurring. We are providing the following information to urge your organization to take action on the safety recommendation in this letter. The Safety Board is vitally interested in this recommendation because it is designed to prevent accidents and save lives.

The NTSB has a reputation for coming up with excellent suggestions for safer transportation. Therefore, whoever receives the recommendation letter usually takes some type of action to improve safety. Often, it takes months or even years before a recommendation leads to action. **Administrative agencies**, politicians, manufacturers, and local governments are often involved. It may require several meetings of government officials or the board of directors of a major company before any changes can be made. This can slow down the process of acting on important safety recommendations.

The NTSB Most-Wanted List

The NTSB often gets behind certain recommendations and continues sending follow-up letters until some action is taken. These follow-up letters provide additional reasons why important safety regulations are necessary. In fact, the NTSB even makes up a most-wanted list. The list is not like the FBI's list of most wanted criminals. Instead, it is a list of the top safety features that the NTSB would like to see go into effect. The list is updated often, since new safety recommendations are made during accident investigations.

An example of a recommendation on the most-wanted list for safety features is one that would help provide safety warnings to airplanes as they move on the ground. Many minor accidents happen while airplanes are **taxiing** along the ground between the airline terminals and the runways. The way it works right now is that all

One of the world's busiest airports, O'Hare in Chicago, Illinois, is undergoing a $1.5 billion expansion project to increase its number of runways. This project followed many accidents that had occurred on the ground as planes taxied on the airport's crowded runway.

communication is between the pilot and the control tower. This works very well when the plane is in the air. But on the ground, the people who are conducting ground traffic, like traffic cops, have to talk to the person in the control tower, who then relays the information to the pilot. This two-step process of relaying information takes 11 seconds. This may be too long to stop two planes from bumping into each other on the ground. The NTSB would like to find a quicker, more direct way for the people handling airport ground traffic to talk directly to the pilots while the planes are on the ground.

An example of a most-wanted safety feature for automobiles would be to have a new law enacted that states that children under a certain age must ride in the back seat. Right now only some states have such a law. The NTSB wants all states to have this law for the safety of young children.

A few of the many recommendations that have been put into action and removed from the most wanted safety feature list include:

- Tougher bus safety standards for school buses

- Stronger penalties for drunk drivers

- Smoke detectors in airline cargo compartments

- New safety laws for passengers in railroad cars

- Automobile child seat-fitting stations, where people can learn the proper way to put a child seat into the car

When the NTSB first started making recommendations, they were a new unknown agency. In 1967, the first year of the NTSB, 36 safety recommendations were made, mostly regarding airline travel. Only one of those was followed. Over the years since, the NTSB has grown to become one of the most respected and important government agencies. In the year 2000, the NTSB made 245 safety recommendations. That year 235 of the NTSB recommendations were

followed. In the years from 1967 through 2001, nearly 12,000 recommendation letters have been issued. Manufacturers, transportation companies, and the agencies that make the laws have followed over 10,000 of those recommendations. That is a very high percentage.

From NTSB Recommendations to Law

Many important NTSB recommendations have become safety laws and safety requirements that we are familiar with today. The NTSB was responsible for many of the safety features for children riding in cars. Child car seats, safer airbags that would not injure a child, door and window locks controlled by the driver, and many other real world features we take for granted were created, or improved because of NTSB recommendations.

The NTSB has tried to improve safety standards for school buses. School bus drivers contend with not only safety concerns, but also with the unpredictable behavior of school students.

Despite the best efforts of the NTSB to eliminate the possibility of accidents related to driver error, accidents will occur. Nevertheless, the NTSB strives to make improved safety its top concern.

Other safety recommendations that have led to real world safety improvements include:

- In 1998, 24-hour toll-free emergency telephone systems were placed on highways at railroad crossings. The recommendation came after highway accidents occurred at railroad crossings.

- On/off switches may now be installed by owners of cars with airbags. The National Highway Traffic Safety Administration followed this recommendation by the NTSB after there were several serious injuries to small children from air bags that were inflated during automobile accidents.

- Drivers' licenses have been changed in most states to include a **graduated license**. This new license includes having a learner's permit, then following special nighttime driving rules before receiving a full license.

- Medications that could make a person too drowsy to operate a vehicle are now labeled with a warning. This recommendation followed accidents in which drivers were too sleepy to drive after taking certain medicines.

It seems that no matter how many safety recommendations the NTSB makes, there is always the need for a new one. New roads, faster vehicles, and new technology make it necessary for the NTSB to keep making new recommendations so that transportation will be safer for the millions of people who travel every day.

One of the more recent threats to automobile safety is the widespread use of cellular phones by drivers. Congress has been inundated with stories of drivers who become careless and distracted by their cellular phone conversations.

CHAPTER 7

Safety Concerns of the Future

TODAY, THERE IS a greater concern for safer transportation than ever before. The NTSB, along with many other government agencies, are working hard to prevent accidents and injuries. There has been great success. For example, statistics show that nearly 85% of people riding in automobiles are wearing seatbelts. The number of highway accidents has decreased in recent years. Accidents caused by drunk drivers have also been lower. But still a lot more can be done to make transportation even safer.

Adjustable Automobile Seats and Correct Use of Car Seats

The NTSB has many recommendations for safety, especially for children. There is a need for child friendly backseats in cars. Often, when children are sitting in the backseats of cars, the seatbelt is not in the right place. The NTSB would like to see seats made so that they can be adjusted for different sized passengers. One car company, Volvo, has created a seat that can be adjusted for the height and size of the passenger. It is hoped that other companies will make similar types of seats. Also, the NTSB has recommended putting shoulder belts in the back seats of cars.

Another area of concern for the future, is car seats for young children. The NTSB has found that 80% of car seats are not used correctly. Either the seat is not strapped into the car correctly, or the child is not safely secured in the seat. Many car dealers and police stations now have **fitting stations,** where people can go to learn how to use cars seats correctly. There are even some fitting stations in vans that park near schools or libraries to teach people how to make the seats as safe as possible. The NTSB is spreading the word and hoping that more fitting stations will be offered and more people will visit them to learn about using car seats correctly.

Cellular Phone Laws

There are also safety concerns about new technology. For example, many states now have laws that do not allow drivers to talk on a cellular phone while driving. Studies will soon show that these laws help prevent accidents. It will not be surprising to see the NTSB recommend stronger laws regarding the use of cellular phones.

Drunken Driving Penalties

Another area of concern continues to be drunk driving. The NTSB wants very strict penalties, called zero tolerance, for drunk driving violations. This means that if a driver has been drinking alcohol, the driver will have his or her license suspended. It is very important not to let people drive if they have been drinking. The NTSB is working hard, recommending that states crack down on drunk driving with stricter penalties.

Some NTSB recommendations are not technical at all, but are very practical ideas. For example, some schools and organizations, such as church groups, transport children in vans instead of school busses. The NTSB would like to see them using school buses, which are built to be safer than vans. Also, other drivers recognize that a school bus is carrying children. They know to drive more carefully around a school bus.

Tightening of Air Safety Measures

Airplane safety will also continue to get a lot of attention from the NTSB and the Federal Aviation Administration. Concerns about noise levels, flight patterns, and passenger safety all are being studied by both agencies. The tragic hijackings of September 11 and the crash of Flight 587 have caused many people to be afraid of flying. Airline companies, together with the Federal Aviation Administration and NTSB, will continue to study many ways to make airline travel as safe as possible so that more people will feel okay about flying. Child seats on airlines may be something we will see in the future. Many other changes to make airplanes safer may not be noticeable to most passengers, but are being considered.

Improvement of Boating Safety

The NTSB is also keeping a watchful eye on boating accidents. They recommend that states make laws that will make sure more people are wearing life jackets. They also recommend that people be taught how to use a life jacket. Many people drown each year because they are not wearing a lifejacket or because they did not put it on correctly. It is also important for anyone operating a boat to have a license and know how to handle the boat. Right now, many states have no boating licenses, which means anybody can take a boat out into the water. The NTSB is working together with the U.S. Coast Guard to improve safety on the water.

Boats are another transportation area in which the NTSB has made recommendations. For example, the NTSB strongly urges the passing of legislation requiring all boaters to wear lifejackets. This photograph illustrates the search for Central Intelligence Agency director, William Colby, who disappeared after a supposed boating accident near his vacation home.

Improvement of Operator Fatigue

Besides coming up with safety ideas for each type of transportation, the NTSB also looks at ways of making all types of transportation safer. For example, there has been a great deal of attention give to the subject of **operator fatigue,** in which a driver, pilot, or engineer is too tired to operate a vehicle safely. The NTSB recommends that people should get at least seven to eight hours of sleep at night if they are going to operate a vehicle. Companies that hire drivers or pilots must make sure to allow them enough hours to get a proper amount of sleep.

Safety First

The suggestions mentioned in this section are just some of the latest concerns of the NTSB. Unlike 20, 30, and 40 years ago when everyone was interested in the fanciest car, biggest plane, or fastest boat, more people today are thinking about safety. The NTSB has set a marvelous example for everyone and made hundreds of recommendations that are now being followed. Despite the fact that one of their most important jobs is to investigate accidents, the NTSB would love it if there were fewer accidents to investigate. They continue to seek ways to make transportation safer for all of us. However, the NTSB cannot do it alone. It is up to everyone to do their part and wear their seatbelts, follow the laws, and do whatever is necessary to travel safely.

Glossary

administrative agencies—group formed, usually by the government, to make sure rules and regulations are made and followed

air traffic controllers—traffic cops of the sky, who make sure airplanes are flying safely and are not near each other

analysis—taking of pieces of information from a whole and studying them carefully

assembly line—an arrangement of workers and parts in which a product such as a car is fully put together piece by piece

black box—an almost indestructible box in which a recording device records everything said by crew in an airplane cockpit

fitting stations—places created to teach people the proper way to use car seats for infants and children

flight data recorder—second black box that tracks information about the engine and instruments

flight pattern—path or direction an airplane is scheduled to follow

gliders—light aircraft without engines, designed to glide or float through the air

graduated license—a special driver's license that begins with a learner's permit, has nighttime driving restrictions, and then progresses to a full license

hijacking—stealing or forcefully taking over an airplane or other vehicle

internal combustion engine—an engine of one or two cylinders in which combustion or heating takes place

interregional—crossing from one region, state, or area to another

mechanical problem—something wrong with a working part or parts of an airplane, car, train, boat, or any machine

news conference—meeting in which a person or persons present information to the news media, including reporters from newspapers, magazines, radio stations, and television stations

Glossary

operator fatigue—state of being too tired to operate a vehicle, including driving a car or bus, flying a plane, engineering a train, and so on

pollution—the process of making air or water dirty by use of chemicals or harmful substances

self-propelled—an object that can move by itself

spokesperson—one person who is selected to speak for the whole group

taxiing—an airplane's slow movement on the ground before or after take off or landing

vehicle—any self-propelled type of transportation that uses wheels

wake turbulence—strong gusty wind that follows an airplane after take off

Further Reading

Ammon, Richard, and Farnsworth, Bill (Illustrator). *Conestoga Wagons.* New York: Holiday House, 2000.

Freedman, Russell. *The Wright Brothers: How They Invented the Airplane.* New York: Holiday House, 1994.

Gourley, Catherine. *Wheels of Time: A Biography of Henry Ford.* Brookfield, CT: Millbrook Press, 1997.

Kent, Zachary. *Charles Lindbergh and the Spirit of St. Louis in American History.* Berkeley Heights, NJ: Enslow Publishers, 2001.

Nahum, Andrew, and King, David (Photographer). *Eyewitness: Flying Machine.* London: Dorling Kindersley Publishing, 2000.

Sherrow, Victoria. *The Exxon Valdez: Tragic Oil Spill.* Berkeley Heights, NJ: Enslow Publishers, 1998.

Index

Airplanes
  and air traffic controllers,
    23, 34
  and American Airlines
    Flight 587, 39-45, 57
  and assistance for victims,
    31, 45
  and black box, 35-36, 41,
    42, 43-44
  and Bureau of Air
    Commerce, 23
  and CAB, 23, 24-25
  and FAA, 24, 25, 29, 30,
    31, 42, 43, 57
  and Grand Canyon, 24
  and hijackings, 24, 35-36,
    37, 57
  history of, 16-17
  and investigations, 27,
    29, 33, 34-36, 37,
    39-45
  judging accidents of, 31
  and laws, 23, 24, 31
  and operator fatigue, 58
  and recommendations,
    47, 49-50, 57
  and reports, 36-37
  and safety measures,
    23-25, 49-50
  and smoke detectors, 50
  and taxiing, 49-50
  and TWA Flight 800, 36
Automobiles
  and airbags, 52
  and cellular phones, 56
  children in, 28, 50, 51,
    52, 55-56
  and drunk drivers, 50, 55,
    56-57

and graduated license, 53
history of, 13-15, 17
and investigations, 27,
  28, 33, 34
and operator fatigue, 28,
  53, 58
and railroad crossings,
  52
and recommendations,
  28, 47, 50, 51-53,
  55-57
and roads, 20-21
and safety measures,
  19-21, 23, 28, 50-53,
  55-58, 56
and seatbelts, 21, 23,
  28, 52

Boats
  and investigations, 27,
    33, 34, 37
  judging accidents of, 31
  and recommendations,
    47, 57
  and U.S. Coast Guard,
    29, 30, 31, 40-41, 57

Carriages, 9-10, 14
Conestoga wagons, 10

Duryea brothers, 13-14

FBI, 30, 37, 42
Ford, Henry, 14-15
Fulton, Robert, 10

Go-Team, 33-36, 39-45

Horses, 9-10, 14

Lindbergh, Charles, 17

Model T, 14

National Conference on
  Street and Highway
  Safety, 19
National Transportation
  Safety Board
  and assistance for victims,
    31, 45
  and cause of accident,
    28, 42-45, 47
  creation of, 25, 27
  and crimes, 25, 37, 42
  funding for, 37
  independence of, 27, 29
  and investigations, 27-31,
    33-36, 39-45
  as judges, 31
  and laws, 28, 31
  and public, 30, 35
  and recommendations,
    28, 30-31, 37, 42-43,
    45, 47-53, 55-59
  and reports, 28, 36-37
  role of, 27-31

Railroads, 11-12, 14, 17,
  27, 29, 33, 34, 47, 50, 58

September 11, terrorist
  attacks of, 37, 40, 57
Steamboats, 10, 14

Trolleys, 12-13

Wright brothers, 16-17

ABOUT THE AUTHOR: Rich Mintzer is the author of 26 non-fiction books including several for children and teens. He has also written articles for national magazines and material for high school students for the Power To Learn website. He has been a professional writer for nearly 20 years and enjoys writing on many different subjects. Rich is currently living in New York City with his wife and two children.

SENIOR CONSULTING EDITOR: Arthur M. Schlesinger, jr. is the leading American historian of our time. He won the Pulitzer Prize for his book *The Age of Jackson* (1945) and again for *A Thousand Days* (1965). This chronicle of the Kennedy Administration also won a National Book Award. Professor Schlesinger is the Albert Schweitzer Professor of the Humanities at the City University of New York and has been involved in several other Chelsea House projects, including the REVOLUTIONARY WAR LEADERS and COLONIAL LEADERS series.

Picture Credits